Disney

Beauty
AND THE
Beast

Level 5

Re-told by: Jane Rollason
Series Editor: Rachel Wilson

T0345640

Contents

In This Book

The Beast

A young prince who is under a magic spell

Belle

An intelligent girl who wants to see the world

Agathe

A poor woman

Gaston

A young man who lives in the same village as Belle

Maurice

Belle's father, who makes music boxes

Cogsworth, Mrs Potts, Lumière, and Plumette

Staff who work at the castle

Before You Read

Introduction

The beast in this story is a handsome prince who lives in a castle. He has rich and beautiful friends but he's not kind. When a poor woman comes to his party, he laughs at her. To his surprise, the woman is an enchantress and she puts a magic spell on him. The prince will look like a beast on the outside until he learns how to love. Can he learn the lesson? Will he stay a beast for ever?

Before You Read

1 **Make sentences.**

1 If you want a book,   **a** you're in a forest.

2 If you're a prince,   **b** you go to prison.

3 If you see a wolf,   **c** you go to a library.

4 If you want a rose,   **d** you live in a castle.

5 If you're a thief,   **e** you go to a garden.

2 *Beauty and the Beast* **is a fairy tale. Which of these things are often true about fairy tales? Choose the best words in italics.**

1 A fairy tale happens *in the past / in the future*.

2 The end of a fairy tale is *happy / unhappy*.

1 The Spell

Once upon a time, a handsome prince lived in a castle. The prince loved parties, but he only invited the most beautiful people in the land.

One evening, the prince had a wonderful party. Outside, the wind was terrible. Suddenly, there was a loud knock at the door. A poor old woman wanted to come in from the storm. She held up a rose to the prince.

The prince laughed loudly and threw her rose on the floor.

Then, in a cloud of gold light, the old woman became a beautiful enchantress.

"You are ugly inside," she said to the prince. "Now you will be ugly outside, too." She put a spell on him and his castle.

The prince changed into a terrible beast. His staff changed into a clock, a candlestick, and a teapot.

"Before the last petal falls from this rose," she said, "you must learn how to love. If another person learns to love *you*, then you can be a prince again."

There was a village near the castle, and the enchantress put a spell on the people there, too. They forgot about the castle and the prince.

A girl called Belle lived in the village. She was kind and intelligent, and dreamed of a life outside of the village. She wanted to travel and see the world, but every day was the same.

The villagers didn't like her. "She's strange," they said. "She's always reading books."

2 Belle

Belle's mother died when she was a baby. Her father Maurice made music boxes to sell at the market in Paris.

The next day was market day so Maurice carefully put his music boxes in a bag. He tied the bag to his horse, Philippe.

"I want to go to the market, too," thought Belle. "But Papa always says no. Perhaps he's right—perhaps the city is too dangerous for me." Belle smiled at her father.

"What shall I bring you?" he asked.

"A rose," said Belle.

Later, Belle went to the village square. First, she bought some bread for a poor woman called Agathe who was often there. Then, Belle did her washing and read her book.

A village girl wanted to see the book, so Belle happily taught her some words.

When the schoolteacher walked by with his class of boys, he saw Belle. "Reading is not for girls!" he shouted.

Some villagers were angry with Belle, so they threw her clean washing on the ground.

"Stop!" shouted a voice. Tall, handsome Gaston rode into the square.

Most of the girls in the village wanted to marry Gaston, but not Belle. He was not a kind man.

"Only the most beautiful girl in the village is good enough for me," he always said. "And that's Belle!"

Belle went home with her dirty washing and Gaston walked beside her.

"When will you marry me, Belle?" he asked.

"Gaston, I will *never* marry you!" she said.

3 The Prison in the Castle

Maurice and Philippe knew the forest well, but now they lost their way. It was summer, but there was ice on the ground and snow on the trees.

Suddenly, Philippe stopped and his ears went back. A gray wolf stood in front of them. There were more wolves in the trees.

"Come on, Philippe," shouted Maurice, turning his horse. They raced through the forest, with the hungry wolves close behind.

They came to a castle. Inside, Maurice found a delicious supper and a warm fire, but no people.

When he sat at the table, something very strange happened. His teacup spoke to him! Maurice was afraid, and he ran outside where Philippe waited.

In the castle garden, he saw some white roses. He remembered the rose for Belle and stopped to get one.

As soon as Maurice cut a rose, he saw a terrible beast.

"You," roared the Beast, "are a thief!"

When Philippe returned home without Maurice, Belle jumped on his back.

"Take me to Papa," she said to the horse.

As soon as Belle was inside the castle, she heard her father's voice. He was at the top of a tower. She ran up the stairs and found him locked in a room. He looked very ill.

Just then, the Beast came and roared at Belle. She was afraid but she didn't run away.

"My father is sick," she said bravely. "He will die in your tower!"

"One of you must stay—you or your father!" roared the Beast. "You can choose."

"Not Belle!" cried Maurice. "I am old. I will stay."

Belle wanted to stay. "Papa will never agree," she thought. Then she had an idea. "Very well," she said. "I will go home. But first, could I kiss him goodbye?"

To Belle's surprise, the Beast agreed to open the door. Could her plan work? She quickly kissed her father, then pushed him out of the room.

"Go home, Papa," she shouted. "I shall take your place."

"No!" cried Maurice.

"He's stupid, and so are you!" said the Beast.

The village tavern was full when Maurice ran in. He told the villagers about the castle, Belle, and the Beast. He told them about the snow and ice, and the teacup that talked.

"Maurice is crazy," laughed the villagers. Gaston laughed with them.

"Please!" shouted Maurice. "Who will help me?"

Then Gaston had an idea and he stopped laughing. "I will help you," he said to Maurice.

4 Wolves

Belle sat sadly in the cold tower.

Suddenly, a clock, a candlestick, and a teapot were outside. To her surprise, they spoke to her! They were very friendly and they opened the door for her.

First, they took her to a beautiful bedroom in the East Tower. Then, they made her a delicious lunch in the kitchen.

"Can I go home?" Belle asked them.

"No, Belle, dear," said the teapot. "I'm sorry."

"Why did you open her door?" roared the Beast.

"It wasn't my idea," said Cogsworth, the clock.

"Maybe she's the one who will break the spell," said Lumière, the candlestick.

"You must ask her to dinner," said Mrs Potts, the teapot.

When the Beast asked Belle to dinner, she said no.

The Beast had a magic mirror. "Show me the girl!" he shouted.

He saw her scared face and he felt sad. A petal fell from the enchantress's rose.

After Belle ate with the staff in the kitchen, she decided to look around the castle.

In the West Tower, she saw the Beast's dirty bedroom. She found the enchantress's red rose, too.

When she tried to touch it, the Beast roared angrily behind her. She was very afraid and ran out of the castle. She found Philippe and they raced away into the dark night.

In the middle of the dark forest, Philippe stopped. It was the wolves! "Help!" cried Belle.

Just then, there was a loud roar. The Beast arrived and fought the wolves. They bit his back and arms, but he was too strong for them. After the wolves ran away, the Beast fell to the ground.

"Shall I leave him?" thought Belle. But she was a kind girl, and she helped him onto Philippe's back. They returned slowly to the castle.

In another part of the forest, Gaston and Maurice couldn't find
the castle.

"I don't believe your story about a beast, old man," Gaston
said angrily. "Where is Belle? She'll soon be my wife, and I want to
find her."

Maurice looked into Gaston's eyes and saw a bad man.
"You'll never marry my daughter," he said.

"Then I'll leave you here for the wolves," laughed Gaston.
He tied poor Maurice to a tree and rode away.

 5 The Library

The Beast was sick and lay asleep. Belle, Mrs Potts, and Lumière sat beside his bed.

"Why do you look after him?" asked Belle.

"He was a lovely little boy," Mrs Potts said. "When his mother died, he was very sad. His father never loved him."

They looked at the rose.

"What happens when the last petal falls?" asked Belle.

"He will stay a beast for all time," said Lumière.

"I'd love to read a book," said Belle.

"Ah," said the Beast. He was not really asleep. "I like reading, too!"

The Beast climbed out of bed. "Come with me," he said to Belle, and he took her to a beautiful library!

"Oh!" said Belle. "What a wonderful place!"

"If you like it so much, it's yours!" smiled the Beast.

Belle and the Beast became friends. They ate, read, and walked around the gardens together.

"Thank you," said Belle one afternoon. "You saved my life."

"And thank *you*," said the Beast. "You didn't leave me to die in the forest."

When Gaston went into the tavern, he was very surprised to see Maurice. Agathe was with him.

"There he is," shouted Maurice, pointing at Gaston. "He left me for the wolves! Ask Agathe! She found me and saved my life!"

The villagers looked at Maurice and they looked at Gaston.

"Who will you believe?" laughed Gaston. "A crazy old man? Or me?"

"We believe *you*, Gaston," one of the villagers said.

"Then we shall take this crazy old man away," said Gaston.

6 The Magic Mirror

There were four petals left on the rose.

"She likes you," Lumière said to the Beast. "Now she must learn to *love* you."

"Ask her to dance," said Mrs Potts.

That evening, the Beast and Belle danced under the stars.

"I would like to see my father," said Belle later.

"I will show you your father," said the Beast, and he brought her his magic mirror. But when Belle looked in the mirror, she cried out.

"Papa! I have to help him!" said Belle.

"You must go to him," said the Beast.

"You mean ... I can leave?" said Belle.

"Yes," said the Beast sadly, "and take the mirror."

Another petal dropped from the rose.

Belle and Philippe raced into the village square.

"My father's not crazy!" shouted Belle. "His story is true!"
She showed them the magic mirror. "Look! There really *is* a Beast."

"Argh!" cried the villagers. When he saw the face of the Beast,
Gaston was afraid.

Gaston took the mirror from Belle. "Look at this animal," he shouted. "Look at his ugly head!"

"No!" answered Belle. "He doesn't frighten me. He's kind ..."

Gaston turned to her. "Perhaps you love this Beast. Or maybe you're crazy like your father. Lock her up with her father!"

"Follow me to the castle!" cried Gaston.

"Kill the Beast!" shouted the villagers.

7 The Fight on the Tower

Belle wanted to help the Beast, but she was locked up with her father. Suddenly, Maurice opened the door. They escaped and Belle rode after the villagers.

The Beast was up on the tower when the angry villagers arrived. The staff were ready. When the villagers came through the front door, they only saw things—a clock, a candlestick, a teapot, a piano, and a chair. But suddenly, these "things" started to fight!

The mirror showed Gaston where the Beast was. He ran up
to the tower. Agathe followed him. Gaston found the Beast.

"Do you really think Belle loves you?" he laughed.

Bang! Gaston shot the Beast, and the Beast fell from the tower.

"No!" cried Belle, behind him. She fought with Gaston, but he
didn't stop.

Gaston found a stone and climbed down toward the Beast.
He tried to hit the Beast, but the Beast easily picked him up.
The Beast was ready to kill Gaston, when he looked again at Belle.
"I am not a beast," he thought, "I am a man." He put Gaston
down. "Go!" he roared.

The Beast climbed higher and came to Belle.

Bang! Bang! Gaston shot the Beast again, twice. But then
Gaston fell off the castle wall ... down and down. He was gone.

The Beast lay on the ground. He was very weak.

"Belle," he said. "I'm dying."

8 The Last Petal

"You came back," the Beast said in a quiet voice.

"Yes!" said Belle. "I'll never leave you again."

His eyes closed. The last petal began to fall from the rose.

"Don't go!" Belle cried. "I love you!"

Suddenly, Agathe was beside them. She looked at Belle and the Beast. She smiled because she was the enchantress. She put her arms above her head and she broke the spell.

The Beast woke up. In a cloud of gold, he began to change into a handsome young prince with lovely blue eyes. Belle and the prince kissed and danced.

Color and summer returned to the castle. Cogsworth, Lumière, and Mrs Potts were people again! The villagers remembered life before the enchantress's spell!

The castle became the happiest home in France.

Belle opened the castle library to the village girls and boys. She taught the girls to read. They could come and read the books any time they wanted.

Belle and the prince lived happily ever after.

After You Read

1 Put the sentences into the correct order.

a The Beast shows Belle the library.

b Belle changes places with Maurice in the Beast's tower.

c The prince has a wonderful party but does not help a poor old woman.

d Gaston falls from the castle wall after he shoots the Beast.

e The enchantress breaks the spell after Belle says, "I love you" to the Beast.

f Belle runs away from the castle, but wolves follow her.

2 Answer the questions.

1 Why does the enchantress change the prince into a beast?

2 Why does Belle dream of a life outside of the village?

3 Why does Gaston decide to help Maurice in the tavern?

4 Why do Belle and the Beast become friends?

5 Why doesn't the Beast kill Gaston?

6 Why does the enchantress change the Beast back into a prince?

3 Discuss the questions with a friend.

1 Who do you like most in the story? Why?

2 Who do you like least in the story? Why?

3 What lesson does this story teach us?

Glossary

beast (*noun*) an animal; a person who is not kind

candlestick (*noun*) a thing that holds candles

crazy (*adj.*) very strange; being ill in your mind

enchantress (*noun*) a woman who can do magic

escape past tense **escaped** (*verb*) to leave a place in a difficult situation; *They escaped and Belle rode after the villagers.*

frighten past tense **frightened** (*verb*) to make a person feel scared; *He doesn't frighten me. He's kind.*

kiss past tense **kissed** (*verb*) to touch someone with your mouth; *She quickly kissed her father, then pushed him out of the room.*

live happily ever after (*phrase*) fairy tales often have a happy ending and they finish with this phrase

lock past tense **locked** (*verb*) to close in; *Belle wanted to help the Beast, but she was locked up with her father.*

magic (*adj.*) having the power to do strange or impossible things

once upon a time (*phrase*) a long time ago; fairy tales usually start with this phrase

petal (*noun*) one of the colored parts on the outside of a flower

roar past tense **roared** (*verb*) to make a very loud noise to frighten a person or because you are angry; *When she tried to touch it, the Beast roared angrily behind her.*

rose (*noun*) a flower with many petals and a sweet smell

spell (*noun*) a piece of magic that a person does; if you put a spell on a person, you do a piece of magic to change them

staff (*noun*) people who work for another person or a business

tavern (*noun*) a place where people go to eat and drink

teapot (*noun*) a thing used to make tea

tie past tense **tied** (*verb*) to hold two things together; *He tied poor Maurice to a tree and rode away.*

wolf (*noun*) an animal that is like a dog and lives in the forest

Play: Books Are for Everyone

Scene 1:

It's morning in a village in France. Belle is walking in the market, reading a book.

BELLE: [reading and thinking to herself]

VILLAGER 1:   [looking at Belle]: Belle's a strange girl. She's always reading.

VILLAGER 2:   Why does she read all the time?

Scene 2:

Later that day, Belle is washing clothes in the village square. She finishes the washing and sits with a girl to teach her to read.

BELLE: [reading slowly]: The blue bird …

GIRL: … f-flies over the d-ar-k, dark wood.

BELLE: Yes! That was wonderful.

A school teacher with a class of boys walks past Belle and the girl.

TEACHER: [to Belle, angrily]: What are you doing? Are you teaching another girl to read? Reading isn't for girls!

VILLAGER 1:   The school teacher is right!

VILLAGER 2:   We have to do something about her!

The Villagers take Belle's washing and throw it on the dirty ground.

BELLE: [Picks up her washing, angrily, and walks away.] I don't care what they say and do. I will make the world a better place.

Scene 3:

Belle now lives in the castle with the Prince. But she never forgets the village children. She invites the girls and boys to the library.

BELLE: You can come as often as you like! If you like a book, you can take it home!

CHILDREN: Hooray!

Global Citizenship

Fighter for Girls at School

Malala Yousafzai grew up in Swat Valley in Pakistan. Her father was a teacher and she loved school.

Then, in 2008, everything changed. A group called the Taliban took power in Swat Valley and they made new laws. People couldn't watch television or listen to music. They closed all the girls' schools.

Malala was a young girl, but she still told her story in newspapers and on television. "Girls want to learn!" she said. The Taliban were angry. One day, in 2012, they attacked her.

Malala survived and went to hospital in England. Now she fights for girls' schools all over the world. More than 130 million girls round the world are not in school today.

Malala won the Nobel Peace Prize in 2014 for her fight for girls.

Why do we read fairy tales?

It's the 21st century! Fairy tales are very old. So why do we still read them?

The First

People told fairy stories over 3,000 years ago. The first time a person wrote one down was in China in 850 AD. It was a *Cinderella* story called Yeh Shen. It's still popular today.

The Longest

The Snow Queen is one of Hans Christian Andersen's longest fairy tales. This story helped inspire the Disney movie *Frozen* (2013).

The Most Popular Animals

Fairy tales are full of frogs, wolves, and cats. Which animal is used the most often? The horse!

Famous Writers

In 1812, German brothers **Jacob and Wilhelm Grimm—The Brothers Grimm—** wrote their first book of fairy tales. They didn't write them for children, and so sometimes very bad things happen in their stories.

Hans Christian Andersen was a Danish writer. He was unhappy when he was a boy. His family was very poor and he had to work in a factory at age 11. Other boys laughed at his strange face and high voice. Some of his tales are about these problems in his early life.

The Lessons

Each fairy tale has a lesson. Here are some:

- *Beauty and the Beast:* beauty is on the inside, not the outside
- *Cinderella*: good things happen when you are kind
- *Little Red Riding Hood*: listen to your parents
- *The Little Mermaid*: follow your dreams

Which of these lessons are important in our lives today, do you think?

Can you think of any other lessons these fairy tales teach us?

century (*noun*) one hundred years. The 21st century is the years 2000 to 2099
popular (*adj.*) when a lot of people like something

Phonics

Say the sounds. Read the words.

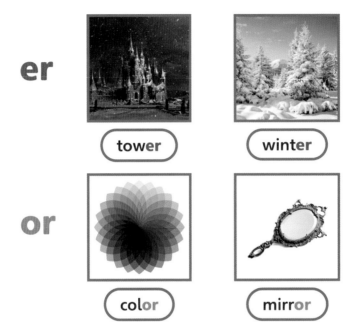

er

(tower)   (winter)

or

(color)   (mirror)

Read, then say the rhyme to a friend.

I'll use the mirror to show me Belle.
Is she the one to break the spell?

Her love could end these years of winter,
And give me back the color of summer.

Can she love me—the Beast in the tower,
Before the last petal falls from the flower?